See, Think, Solve:

A Simple Way To Tackle Tough Problems

Andrew Benedict-Nelson & Jeff Leitner

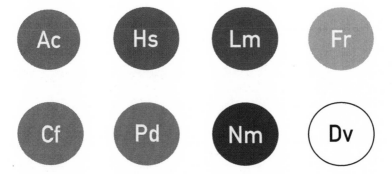

Grateful acknowledgment is made for the permission to use concepts from Innovation Dynamics © 2016 by The Brador Group, Ltd.

To Marilyn Flynn, Annalisa Enrile, and Nadia Islam,
our partners in thought.

Table of Contents

Section 2: Think

Section 3: Solve

Introduction

The world is full of problems. There are probably more problems in the world than there are people.

Everybody wants to solve the problems around them to make life better for themselves and others. Yet most people can't figure out where to start. A lot of times, they can't even see where their problem ends and other problems begin.

In this book, you'll learn about nine steps that will make it easier to see and understand the problems around you. They are drawn from the authors' experience helping people reckon with tough problems all over the world.

Before we begin, let's briefly consider what really makes a problem hard.

Some problems are easy to solve, like $2 + 2 = 4$.

But most problems are harder than that. They have many possible answers, and it is often hard to tell when you have actually solved them.

The main reason problems are hard to solve is that they involve people.

People are funny. They don't always believe the things they say they believe or do the things they say they are going to do. They can act one way in one situation and act completely differently in another situation. No one has ever completely figured this out. We call this the "mystery of human behavior."

The mystery of human behavior shapes almost every problem worth solving. That's the bad news. But there's good news too. The mystery of human behavior also helps us see problems in new ways. By paying attention to people, we can discover new aspects of problems that help us solve them more effectively.

The nine steps in this book are designed to do just that. They will help you make sense of the mystery of human behavior that surrounds all tough problems.

The first six steps are about seeing — each of them shows you a new thing to look for in human behavior.

The next two steps are about thinking — each one is a tool you can use to better understand the human behaviors you have observed.

The last step is about solving — it describes what you can accomplish with your newfound knowledge.

In the course of each chapter, you will be asked to picture various kinds of people solving problems in scenes from everyday life.

Once you've finished a chapter, talk a look around and you'll see all sorts of aspects of human behavior you didn't see before.

The more you practice following these steps, the better you'll be at using them to solve any kind of problem, anywhere.

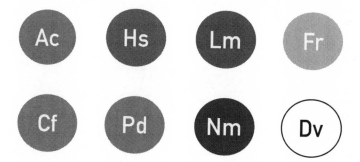

See

Ac

Hs

Lm

Fr

Cf

Pd

Nm

Dv

Section 1: See

This section is about six things to look for to help you understand and solve problems. These things are all around you all the time, but seeing them requires practice.

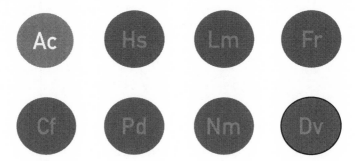

Chapter 1: See Actors

As we said, almost all problems involve people. You can better understand those people if you understand the different ways they interact with your problem. To do this, think of the people as "actors."

By actors, we don't mean movie stars. "Actors" means any people or group of people who play a role in your problem.

There are three kinds of actors:

▸ first-order actors, who play a direct role in a problem;

▸ second-order actors, who influence the first-order actors; and

▸ missing actors, who shape the problem by not being there.

Don't worry, we'll go through these one at a time.

A first-order actor is anyone who plays a direct role in a problem.

Picture a car accident.

That is definitely a problem. Fortunately, it is just a fender bender and no one got hurt.

There are lots of first-order actors in this problem: the drivers, the passengers, the bystanders who witnessed the accident, and the police officer who writes up a report.

There are even less obvious first-order actors, like the insurance company that will be helping to fix the damage caused by the collision.

Notice that each of these first-order actors is directly involved in the problem and has a very specific role to play.

Picture a corner grocery store.

The owner of the store is trying to solve the problem of providing food to her customers while supporting her family.

There are lots of other first-order actors – shoppers, checkout clerks, and suppliers to name a few.

Each of the first-order actors plays a role in the store's success or failure.

But there are other first-order actors you don't see at first, like the people who walk right by the store to shop at a competitor.

These would-be customers are important actors and could have a lot to do with the owner's success or failure.

But not all actors are first-order actors. Let's look at the other kinds.

Second-order actors are not directly involved in the problem, but they influence the ones who are.

Picture a group of kids studying in the school library.

They are trying to solve the problem of passing a test. The kids are obviously first-order actors. So is the instructor who taught them the material and the librarian who makes sure they have a quiet place to study.

But there's an important second-order actor in this problem: the kids' parents. While the parents aren't directly involved with the problem of passing the test, they undoubtedly influence the other actors who are — most notably, their kids.

First-order actors aren't more important than second-order actors, and second-order actors aren't more important than first-order actors. They're just different, in that they play very different roles in a problem.

Now, let's look at the last category of actors: missing actors. Missing actors are the people you might expect to be involved, but aren't.

Picture a dog scaring an old lady in a park.

There are many first-order actors here: the scared woman, her friends, the men running after the dog, and the animal control truck racing to the scene.

But this imaginary dog running loose in this imaginary park has a collar and license. This suggests that there's an important missing actor: the dog's owner who isn't there.

Missing actors influence the problem by not being there.

Now that you are beginning to see actors, here is something else to think about. All actors in all problem have their own interests and motivations. If you can envision those interests and motivations, you can begin to understand why they do what they do.

Remember...

▸ Actors are people or groups who play a role in your problem.

▸ There are three kinds of actors:

  ▸ first-order actors, who play a direct role in your problem;

  ▸ second-order actors, who influence the first-order actors; and

  ▸ missing actors, who shape your problem by not being there.

▸ Every actor has his or her own motivation and interests.

Questions to Help You See

▸ What people or groups are directly involved in your problem?

▸ Who influences the people or groups directly involved in your problem?

▸ Who plays an important role by not being around?

▸ What are the motivations or interests of people directly involved in your problem?

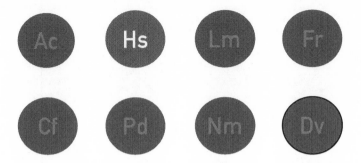

Chapter 2: See History

Every problem has a past. Most problems you encounter in the world have been around in some form or another for years or even generations. The problem's past is captured in its "history" — though that word doesn't mean what you probably think it means.

History isn't definitive or absolute. Yes, we know that's an odd idea, but one of us was trained as a historian, so we promise it's true.

Instead, history is a collection of stories about the problem's past - the official stories, the unofficial stories, the half-truths and the you've-got-to-be-kidding-me stories.

Picture a group of people cleaning graffiti from a big statue in a neighborhood park.

To them, this graffiti is a big problem — they are offended that anyone would tag the statue, because it commemorates their ancestors who died in a war.

Now picture the kids who spray-painted the statue.

They don't know anything about the war or the ancestors. To them, the statue is just the tallest thing in the neighborhood. Each group of actors has their own stories.

Picture some kids waiting on a bench near a parking lot.

They are going from their mother's house to their father's house for the weekend. Mom and Dad got divorced five years ago. As you might expect, each parent has his or her own version of what happened.

But there are even more stories about this problem.

For example, each of the kids probably has his or her own version of the story, which likely includes elements of Mom's story and Dad's story. The judge who rules on the divorce has his own version of the story based on what he thinks are the objective facts.

Remember, even untrue stories and myths are part of a problem's history.

Picture an old playground in a park.

Besides being old, the playground has one noticeable feature: all the playground equipment is blue and white.

The town council is reviewing proposals to update the playground. The council members are pretty open to new ideas, as long as the playground equipment remains blue and white.

You see, blue and white are the colors of the local high school, which all the council members attended. They all believe, in fact, that the playground's colors are some kind of commemoration of a big football victory many years ago.

But none of that is actually true. The truth is that there was a fire many years ago, which singed the equipment. The fire department, which volunteered to repaint the playground equipment, could only track down blue and white paint.

What's important here is not actually what happened, but what everybody believes happened. That's how the history of problems works.

Now that you're beginning to see history, let us warn you about something important: it is not your job to figure out who's right and who's wrong. It doesn't matter, exactly.

What matters is what all the stories — the true ones, the false ones, the somber ones, and the silly ones — tell you about the actors involved.

Remember...

▸ History is a collection of stories about your problem's past.

▸ All kinds of stories are important to history, including true stories, false stories, half-truths, and nonsense stories.

▸ It's not your job to determine which stories are true; it's your job to gather as many stories as you can to help you understand your problem.

Questions to Help You See

▸ How do people say your problem started?

▸ How do people explain why your problem is still around?

▸ What would people say are the most important events in your problem's story?

▸ What falsehoods do people spread about your problem?

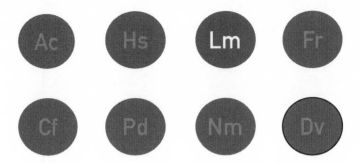

Chapter 3: See Limits

Every problem is bound by rules, which we call
"limits." Limits are the formal, explicit rules that
influence how people behave in relation to a
problem.

Sometimes, people follow the rules. Sometimes, people break the rules and sometimes, those people experience consequences.

Sometimes, the rules are easy to break, like the speed limit. Other times, the rules are impossible to break, like the law of gravity.

In any event, watching how actors respond to limits can tell you a lot about problems.

Picture kids at the neighborhood pool.

They are trying to solve the problem of having fun on a summer day. But the pool has lots of rules. If the kids start throwing each other into the pool, the lifeguard will probably reprimand them. If a kid dives into the shallow end, the lifeguard might ban her for the day. If a kid pees in the pool, everyone has to get out.

Most everyone understands that these are the rules of the pool. They shape the way people behave there, and most everyone would follow them even if there were no lifeguard around. The pool has a well-established set of limits that most people follow.

But sometimes there are limits that everyone knows and no one follows.

Picture those same kids at an empty beach.

There is a big sign warning that there should be no swimming when no lifeguard is present. But the city stopped enforcing that rule a long time ago, so everybody just ignores the big sign and swims anyway. They treat the limits of the beach differently than the limits of the pool, probably because no one they know has ever followed the rule on the big sign.

You can learn a lot about limits by watching how actors respond to them.

For example, picture a mom arguing with her son in their driveway.

She is trying to solve the problem of making her son a safer driver.

She says he needs to be more careful when he drives around the neighborhood. He says that he is a good driver because he always stops at stop signs. "That's easy," Mom says. "But you should follow the speed limit, too."

"But you don't follow the speed limit, Mom!" the kid says. "Just the other day, you drove ten miles over the speed limit on the highway."

"Okay, that's true," Mom says, "but I saw you driving ten miles over the limit around our block the other day. Kids play in the street here — you need to be more careful."

Apparently, not all speed limits are created equal. Just because a limit is obeyed in one situation doesn't mean it will be obeyed in another situation.

There are lots of kinds of limits. Some limits result from limited resources, like budgets for money and schedules for time. Some limits are part of the natural world, like cold in the winter and dry in the desert.

Limits are any formal, explicit rule actors have to take into account, whether they are naturally occurring or artificial.

Let's return to the mom trying to make her son a safer driver. The first time there is a bad snow, she insists on driving with him. He may think he can drive in the snow, but there are lots of new behaviors he needs to adopt in response to the change in limits. For example, Mom tells him to drive in the tracks of the cars in front of him so he doesn't skid out. This is a common response to the limit of snowy roads.

Picture a house party.

The organizers are very friendly people and want to solve the problem of including as many people from the neighborhood as possible. But their living room is only so big. After a few dozen people show up, they have to start turning people away. Maybe next time they'll find a bigger location with different limits.

Picture an amusement park.

A line of kids want to get on the park's scariest roller coaster. They are trying to solve the problem of having as much fun as they can while they are at the park. But the attendant turns some of the smaller kids away, pointing to a sign that says they need to be at least five feet tall to ride.

The park turns these kids away because of a natural limit — centrifugal force could throw the smaller kids off the ride. But because no one wants to argue physics with a nine-year-old, they made a sign with a rule and told their attendants to carefully enforce it. Lots of limits work this way.

Now that you're beginning to see limits, here's
something else to think about: what really matters
about limits is how actors respond to them. Do they
follow the rules? Do they break the rules? Do they
ignore the rules? Do they outright change the rules?

Those behaviors will tell you a whole lot about the
problem you're trying to understand.

Remember...

▸ Limits are the formal, explicit rules that influence how people behave in relation to your problem.

▸ Limits can be naturally occurring, like gravity, or people-made, like the speed limit.

▸ Actors do all sorts of things with limits, including follow them, break them, ignore them, and change them.

Questions to Help You See

▸ What are some of the rules and laws that
influence how people behave around your
problem?

▸ Which rules related to your problem do people
usually follow and which ones do they usually
ignore?

▸ How do people respond to limits of time and
money related to your problem?

▸ What laws of nature are specifically related to
your problem?

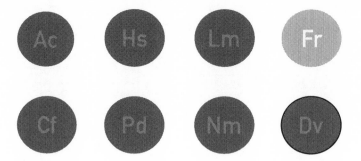

Chapter 4: See Future

Of course, nobody can accurately predict the future. But everybody thinks about it all the time, particularly when we're trying to solve tough problems.

This constant calculating about what will happen next is what we mean by "future." In other words, we're not interested in what will happen as much as we are in what people think will happen.

Future is the collection of people's expectations about how a problem will turn out.

Picture a father and his daughter planning an outing to a concert in the park.

They are trying to solve the problem of bringing everything they need for the event. Dad is bringing an umbrella in case it rains. The daughter isn't bringing an umbrella because she's sure it won't.

They believe different things about the future.

Picture a couple waiting for a bus.

They are trying to solve the problem of getting to the other side of town. Unfortunately, the bus does not show up at its scheduled time. One member of the couple believes that the late bus will never come. So he suggests they start walking. The other member of the couple believes that the late bus will be there shortly. So he suggests they just wait. They have a loud argument about the future.

Sometimes, the future surprises everybody. Sometimes, things we never thought would take place happen. Sometimes, things we were certain would happen never do.

Again, what's interesting about future is what actors expect.

Picture a parking lot.

It's empty now, but for years, it was where people bought fireworks for their independence day celebrations. Everybody in the neighborhood assumed the fireworks tent would be there the next time they tried to solve the problem of buying fireworks.

But the woman who sold fireworks retired and didn't bother to tell anyone. The future seemed certain and then wasn't.

Picture a baker coming home from a long day making bread.

He's barely making ends meet and has started to make plans to move away and find another job.

Little does he know that tonight at a party, he will meet a cake decorator and fall madly in love. The two of them will ultimately open a shop together, which will become the neighborhood hotspot. But tonight, he sees no future for himself at all.

Now that you're beginning to see actors'
expectations about the future, you can begin to sort
them into some common categories. We like to think
about things being likely to happen, unlikely to
happen, or impossible to happen.

Remember, it's not important whether the actors you're watching are right. It's only important that you understand how they see the world.

Remember...

▸ Future is the collection of people's expectations about how your problem will turn out.

▸ Beliefs about the future don't have to be right to influence how actors behave.

▸ It's helpful to sort expectations into likely, unlikely, and impossible.

Questions to Help You See

▸ What is the most common belief about the future of your problem?

▸ What do people believe is possible, but unlikely to happen with your problem?

▸ What single event might people say would change the future of your problem?

▸ What do people believe could never, ever happen in the future of your problem?

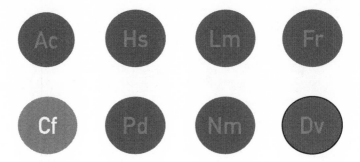

Chapter 5: See Configuration

There is an overwhelming, ever-growing amount of information in the world. There's so much that if we didn't have some intuitive sense of how to sort through it, we'd probably go insane.

That's configuration – all the labels and categories people use to make sense of a problem.

Configuration is a fancy word, so it sounds like it might be complicated. It's not. You and everybody else do it all the time without recognizing it. You just need to look for it.

Picture a family's laundry room.

One of the kids has come home from college with a bunch of dirty laundry, so he's sorting it into lights and darks.

You no doubt recognize this as a common configuration related to the problem of doing laundry.

Picture a pair of garbage cans on the corner.

One is for trash that will go to the landfill; the other is for materials that will go to the recycling center.

You surely recognize this too, as a common configuration related to the problem of cleaning up.

The laundry and garbage configurations are pretty obvious. One is based on common sense and experience (laundry) and the other by explicit signage (garbage).

But lots of other configurations shape our lives in less obvious ways.

Picture a potter.

For years she has crafted mugs and vases for friends as gifts. Now she is hoping to rent the ground floor apartment of her building and turn it into a shop. This will help her solve the problem of simultaneously pursuing her passion and making a living.

Unfortunately, the potter finds out that her town has zoning laws that prevent her from opening a retail business in her apartment building. The zoning configuration will force her to move.

Picture some railroad tracks.

Many years ago, people who lived on one side of the tracks looked down on people who live on the other side. They said people on the other side were uncouth and different.

These days, most people in town have friends on both sides. Younger residents and newcomers may not even know this historic configuration exists.

But it still affects how some older residents think about the neighborhood and how to solve its problems.

Here's a weird thing about configuration: all configurations are just categories that people made up.

Configuration doesn't occur in nature. The categories we associate with nature – like animal, vegetable, and mineral – were just invented by zoologists, botanists, and geologists to help them make sense of the world.

Configuration is really powerful. It has to be if it's going to be useful in helping us sort through all the information in the world.

But like everything powerful, sometimes people use it in ways that make sense and sometimes people use it in ways that just seem silly.

Picture a middle-aged couple listening to the radio.

The station plays a song from the 1960s that they both sing along to.

Then the station plays a song from the 1970s. The man says, "This song doesn't belong on the oldies station – it's classic rock."

After that, the station plays a song from the 1980s. The woman says, "This song doesn't belong on this station – it's too recent."

Across town, an ad executive who bought time on the station because it reaches his target demographic doesn't care what songs the station plays. He doesn't care if they rebrand themselves as "adult alternative."

Now that you're beginning to see configuration, you will probably start to see it everywhere. You will see the big effect it has on people's behavior. You may even want to free people of those effects by screaming at them "This stuff is all just made up!"

But that's not your job. The most useful thing you can do when you see a configuration shaping people's behavior is to understand why it came to exist in the first place.

In particular, consider what problems people were trying to solve when the configuration was originally invented. Even strange and arbitrary configurations were usually invented for some reason. Investigate that to better understand your problem.

Remember...

▸ Configuration is the labels and categories people use to make sense of your problem.

▸ Every configuration is just something somebody made up to solve a problem.

▸ Sometimes, people use configuration in a way that makes sense (laundry) and sometimes, people use it in a way that doesn't (categories of music).

Questions to Help You See

▸ What official labels or categories do people use when talking about your problem?

▸ What informal labels or categories do people use when talking about your problem?

▸ What labels or categories might you use when describing your problem to an outsider?

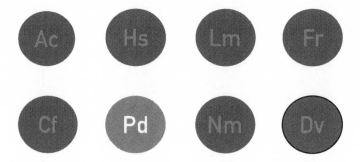

Chapter 6: See Parthood

It would be nice if tough problems were well-organized and clearly defined. But part of what makes tough problems tough is that the problems are all jumbled up together. To make sense of the resulting mess, we look for a thing called "parthood."

Parthood is the relationship a problem has to other problems.

Picture a gate at an airport.

All the would-be passengers are frustrated because the flight is an hour late. One passenger in particular is really angry, complaining loudly about how he is going to miss his important meeting. "Why is this flight late? There's no bad weather anywhere on the map."

Notice how the angry passenger naturally understood parthood. The problem of flight delays is usually jumbled up with the problem of bad weather.

But in this instance, the flight delay had nothing to do with bad weather. The angry passenger was right: there was no bad weather anywhere in the country.

There was, however, a terrorist threat in an airport a thousand miles away. This shut down air travel everywhere, saving lives but inconveniencing the angry passenger. This time, the problem of flight delays was mixed up with the problem of national security.

Picture a busy road running through a neighborhood where lots of children live.

Some parents want to solve the problem of child safety by reducing the speed limit, adding stop signs, and doubling the number of crosswalks.

But City Hall turns down their request. It turns out that the same road is used by hundreds of drivers each week to get to a nearby mall. The parents don't know it, but their problem of child safety is all mixed up with the problems of traffic congestion and retail business.

Picture a roadside fruit stand.

After several years of struggling to make ends meet, the owner is about to give up and shut down. But then he starts getting many more customers than usual.

It turns out that a recording artist who grew up nearby used a picture of the fruit stand on the cover of his new album. The recording artist was trying to solve the problem of showing he was authentic.

The owner of the fruit stand doesn't care about the recording artist's problem, but he's grateful for the additional business. In fact, he starts selling T-shirts with a picture of his fruit stand to tourists.

Once you begin to get good at seeing parthood, you will also see that it never really ends. Every problem is part of every other problem – sometimes, in ways that are very hard to see.

But there are some clues to look for. One, look to see if your problem and another problem share actors (like drivers in the story about the road). Two, look to see if your problem and another problem share settings (like the fruit stand). Finally, look to see if your problem and another problem share resources (like airplanes in the story about the delayed flight).

Remember...

▸ Parthood is the relationship your problem has to other problems.

▸ Parthood is infinite – all problems are related to all other problems somehow.

▸ Problems are often related through shared actors, shared settings, or shared resources.

Questions to Help You See

▸ What problems are obviously related to your problem?

▸ What other problems would outsiders be surprised are related to your problem?

▸ What other problems do actors in your problem worry about?

▸ What other problems would disappear if your problem were resolved?

Think

Section 2: Think

This section is about two things to think about to help you understand and solve problems. They can be hard to get your head around, but the six things from the previous section will help you.

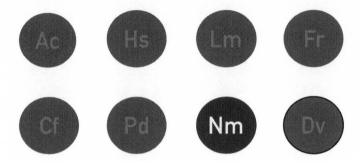

Chapter 7: Think About Norms

The six things you learned to look for in the previous chapters are useful in themselves. But they are even more useful in helping you think about something really important called social norms.

Social norms are unspoken, informal rules that tell everybody how to behave in social situations.

As there are a gazillion different social situations, there are many gazillion different social norms.

There are norms that tell people how to behave on the subway and norms that tell people how to behave at the dinner table. There are norms for the office and norms for the ballgame. For every situation that involves people, there are social norms.

Social norms are invisible.

People around us send us subtle signals they don't even know they're sending that we process without even knowing we're processing.

Here's an example: Everybody who gets on an elevator turns around and faces the door. There's no law about this and there's no sign telling you to do it. But everybody does it because it's a social norm, because the other people on the elevator are sending us subtle signals to turn around.

Don't believe us? Just try to face everybody else on the elevator and grin all the way down to the lobby. It will make you and your fellow passengers really uncomfortable. That discomfort tells you it's a social norm.

Social norms are crazy powerful.

Social scientists now believe that norms are a bigger influence on how people behave than any other single factor, including character, childhood, or brain chemistry.

Social norms can change.

Not too long ago, nobody in polite society ever put his or her elbows on the dinner table. A man never wore a hat indoors. Those two informal rules aren't such a big deal anymore.

The fact that norms can change is a big deal when you're tackling people problems. But we'll get to that in the last chapter.

Remember how we said social norms are invisible? That's where actors, history, limits, future, configuration, and parthood come in.

The six things you've learned to look for in the first six chapters give you clues to norms you can't see.

▸ You can see how actors behave.

▸ You can listen to the stories about the problem that people tell.

▸ You can see how people act in response to limits.

▸ You can look at people's expectations about the future.

▸ You can listen for how people describe your problem with categories.

▸ You can see what other problems are mixed up in your problem.

And all that seeing, listening, and looking are clues to social norms.

Let's look back at the some of the social situations you've already read about in this book and think about some norms.

In chapter 1, there was a dog scaring an old woman in a park.

There were lots of bystanders rushing to help, but the dog's owner was not on the scene. You could imagine the neighbors who helped chastising or shunning the dog's owner for violating the social norm of "if you own a dog, keep it under control."

In chapter 3, a mother was trying to teach her son to be a better driver.

She explained to him that it's more important to follow speed limits in the neighborhood than on the highway. She was reinforcing the social norm of "drive more carefully in residential areas where children live."

In chapter 5, there were two garbage cans on the corner – one for trash and one for recycling.

This is a pretty clear indication of the social norm of "you should do your part to help the environment."

Social norms like these are at the heart of all tough problems.

The key to solving those problems is recognizing and thinking about the norms.

Remember...

▸ Social norms are unspoken, informal rules that tell everybody how to behave in social situations.

▸ Social norms are the single biggest influence on how people behave.

▸ Social norms are invisible, but you gather clues about them by looking at your problem's actors, history, limits, future, configuration, and parthood.

Questions to Help You Think

▸ What are the social situations you most associate with your problem?

▸ What do actors do in relation to your problem that can't be explained by laws or formal, explicit rules?

▸ Somebody keeps actors related to your problem in line. Who is it?

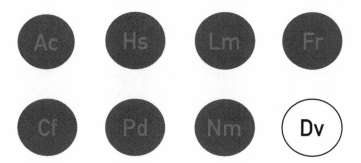

Chapter 8: Think About Deviance

Human behavior is mysterious in part because it's always changing. Sometimes, the change is trivial, like the lengths of hemlines. Sometimes, the change is earth-shaking, like people's fundamental beliefs about the origin of the Universe. All told, human behavior varies gigantically over different times and different places.

In the previous chapter, you learned about a big idea to help you make sense of that mysterious behavior: social norms. As you'll recall, norms are unspoken, informal rules that tell women what length skirt to wear this season and what beliefs about the origin of the Universe it's wise to articulate in public.

Here's another big idea to help you think about the mysteries of human behavior: deviance.

Deviance is a behavior with the potential to subvert a social norm.

In other words, deviant behavior is so disruptive that it doesn't just break the rules, it can change the rules altogether.

This point is so important we want to make it again. Deviance is not just breaking the rules. It's breaking the rules so hard or so cleverly that it changes the rules.

Almost everywhere, being faithful to your spouse is a social norm. And almost everywhere, there are plenty of people violating that norm.

But notice that the norm stays intact no matter how many people break it. Cheating on your spouse may be wrong, but it is not a deviance.

On the other hand, families eating dinner together used to be a pretty universal social norm. But along came behaviors related to new technologies like TV and smartphones. Now fewer and fewer families regularly eat dinner together.

The new behaviors were so powerful that they altered a long-standing social norm.

Let's look back at some of the social situations in this book and think about deviance.

In chapter 2, kids had spray-painted graffiti on a statue in the park.

And as you'll recall, older residents were offended by it, as the statue commemorated their ancestors who died in a war. The social norm was obviously "honor our ancestors who fought for us in wars."

But imagine that the graffiti read "war criminal!" Imagine that the graffiti sparked a few local residents to do more research into what those ancestors did in the war and then start a petition to take the statue down. That could challenge and ultimately change the social norm.

In chapter 4, the town's fireworks tent was shut down.

Everybody in the neighborhood was surprised because the owner didn't bother to tell anyone. So much for the social norm of parents and kids going together to buy fireworks each July.

But imagine that one fireworks aficionado in town didn't care at all because he had been buying fireworks online for years. In fact, the tent's former owner had seen the handwriting on the wall when she decided to retire. The deviance of buying fireworks online doomed fireworks tents like hers.

In chapter 6, parents discovered that their efforts to solve the problem of child safety were tied up with the problem of traffic flow toward a popular mall.

You'll recall that City Hall rejected their request for a reduced speed limit, more stop signs, and additional crosswalks.

But imagine if the parents challenged the social norm of "defer to the needs of local businesses." Imagine if they started a boycott of the mall and launched a social media campaign alleging that the mall's owners don't care about local children. You can imagine how the mall and other businesses might begin to invest in child safety, changing the local norm for good.

One last note about deviance: it is neither objectively good nor objectively bad. Were the kids right to paint "war criminal!" on the statue? Were the parents right to boycott the mall?

Of course, it's hard to say; it depends on your point of view. But what isn't hard to say is that social norms were changed.

Remember...

▸ Deviance is a behavior with the potential to subvert a social norm.

▸ You can piece together clues to see and think about social norms. But for deviance, you have to use your imagination.

▸ Deviance is neither objectively good nor objectively bad.

Questions to Help You Think

▸ What social norms related to your problem need changing?

▸ Is there an existing behavior out there that could ultimately change the norms related to your problem?

▸ Can you imagine a new behavior that could ultimately change the norms related to your problem?

Solve

Ac Hs Lm Fr

Cf Pd Nm Dv

Section 3: Solve

This section is about how to use everything you learned in the previous two sections to solve tough problems.

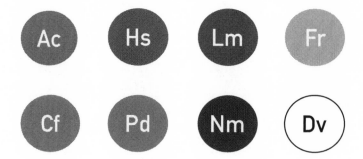

Chapter 9: Social Change

This book is like a jigsaw puzzle. Over the previous chapters, you've learned about eight puzzle pieces: six thing to look for to help you understand the problems you're trying to solve and two things to think about to make sense of those problems.

Now it's time to assemble the puzzle.

The eight pieces fit together in an approach to solving tough problems – specifically, an approach to designing solutions to complex people-related problems.

Just as you would with any puzzle – after you spilled out the pieces and before you began trying to fit them together – you look at the picture on the box. Let's look at what this approach will look like when you're done.

Here is the most important sentence in the book:

Every tough problem is held in place by one or more problematic social norms.

To make sure you're following us, let's break that sentence down.

▸ "Every tough problem" - As we've discussed, tough problems are mainly tough because they involve people and the mystery of human behavior.

▸ "is held in place" - Tough problems are there for you to solve because they don't go away by themselves and have successfully resisted solutions for years or even generations.

▸ "by one or more problematic social norms" - There are informal, unspoken rules that are undermining efforts to solve the problem for good. In other words, people are being encouraged to behave in ways that perpetuate the problem or keep solutions from sticking – likely without even knowing it.

So that there's no ambiguity, problematic social norms are why societies struggle to eradicate homelessness, eliminate hunger, and end war. Unhealthy social norms are why companies can't get employees on the same page and why legislative bodies stop working effectively.

The root cause of these and all other tough problems is unhealthy norms. The solution is new, healthier norms.

This approach to solving tough problems is about replacing old norms with new norms. That's the picture on the box.

Now that you know what you're going to build with the eight puzzle pieces, let's look at them again.

The first six pieces – actors, history, limits, future, configuration, and parthood – are what you need to unearth problematic norms. Remember, norms are crazy powerful but invisible. You can't see norms just by looking at a problem. You need the six pieces to gather clues.

The seventh piece is old norms. This is the root cause of your problem. You will piece together the clues you gather with the first six pieces to find one or more problematic, unhealthy norms.

The final piece is deviance. Deviance is how you create new, healthier norms. Using the clues you picked up with actors, history, limits, future, configuration, and parthood, you'll either find or imagine a behavior so powerful that it could subvert the problematic, unhealthy norms.

Now let's walk through a problem together so you can see how this approach works.

We'll look back more than a century to the beginning of urban poverty in America.

After the Civil War, the country transitioned from an economy driven by agriculture to an economy driven by industrial production. This change lured millions of Americans to cities for work, but there they found inadequate housing, inadequate food, and crime. By the turn of the century, Americans were aware of this new challenge, thanks to popular books like *How the Other Half Lives* by Jacob Riis and *The Jungle* by Upton Sinclair.

Actors

Many first-order actors were connected to this new problem of urban poverty. Obviously, there was the poor, themselves. There were newly-wealthy industrialists who relied on the poor for cheap labor. There were slumlords who exploited the poor for rent. There were bosses of political machines who exploited the poor for votes. And there was the growing number of Americans who were distressed by what they read and heard about urban poverty and were looking for ways to help.

There were important second-order actors. Most of the people who came to the aid of the poor were upper-class women influenced by charismatic Christian preachers, progressive philosophers, and muckraking journalists. These upper-class women often sought to help the poor by filling in for missing actors – serving as "friendly visitors" who could teach the poor the middle-class virtues and habits they allegedly lacked.

History

You already know part of the history of this problem. For the country's first 100 years, most Americans thought of themselves as a rural people whose lives were tied intimately to the land. Many people were born, lived, and died in the same village or town. Furthermore, the ideal American was usually portrayed as a person of Northern European descent.

But the growing population of the nation's cities were largely immigrants from Eastern and Southern Europe. African-Americans were also migrating north and Hispanic and Asian populations were increasing in the West. The story of America as a white, rural nation was being challenged.

Limits

If you look at the limits surrounding the urban poor in this time period, you'll mainly notice what there isn't: no laws against child labor, no compulsory school attendance, no workplace safety laws, and no fair housing standards.

Courts and police frequently backed up the rich in disputes with the poor over labor or crime. The nation's immigration laws in this time also demonstrated a new obsession with keeping America's population "pure." Between 1802 and 1870, no major immigration laws were passed in the United States. But in 1882, the Chinese Exclusion Act first created the category of "illegal immigrant." Later laws sought to curtail immigration through increased enforcement and new quotas.

Future

To the upper class at the turn of the century, the future of many of America's cities looked bleak. This is best seen through the huge interest at the time in eugenics, which purported to be a scientific approach to racial improvement. Eugenicists looked at the future and insisted that the "right kind" of Americans (i.e., wealthy people of Northern European stock) needed to have more children and the "wrong kind" of Americans (i.e., everybody else), needed to have fewer.

If this didn't happen, eugenicists believed, American civilization would decline. Supreme Court Justice Oliver Wendell Holmes spoke for the majority of upper-class Americans when he wrote in an opinion supporting the compulsory sterilization of a poor woman that "Three generations of imbeciles are enough."

Configuration

The changing cities of the turn of the century brought new configurations. Americans began to see cities as divided up into different sections based on ethnicity and class. There was an increase in institutions designed to manage the problems of urban poverty, including poorhouses, reform schools, tenements, orphanages, and asylums. Everyone understood these to be charitable institutions governed by the rich and used by the poor.

Of course, "rich" and "poor" themselves, as well as all ethnicities, are also configurations. Many Americans further subdivided people in poverty into the "worthy poor" (able-bodied people deserving of assistance) and the "unworthy poor" (people who could not or would not work, including alcoholics and the mentally ill).

Parthood

As for parthood, there were a lot of problems that privileged Americans associated with urban poverty. The most obvious was disease. The new public health departments of the time frequently blamed problems like cholera and tuberculosis on the poor. It was not by accident that people then were fascinated by the story of "Typhoid Mary," a poor Irish cook in New York who was naturally immune to typhoid fever but spread the disease to several rich families. It was completely normal for Americans at this time to believe that the problems of poverty and infectious disease went hand in hand.

Norms

A look back at the beginning of urban poverty in America through actors, history, limits, future, configuration, and parthood reveals a lot of social norms. Among them is one norm that was especially problematic: the rich should be separated from the poor.

This had not always been a norm. While social class had always been part of the American life, rich and poor had been likely to mix in settings like the village church or the town hall meeting.

But now, rich and poor were becoming more like different nations side by side, exacerbating urban poverty and every problem connected to it. Some of the wealthy felt a sense of duty towards the poor, but they could only imagine helping them as benighted foreigners, not as fellow citizens. It was entirely normal for rich elites at the time to expect and demand that their homes and bodies remain far away from what they believed were the dirty, diseased ghettos of major cities.

Deviance

Then deviance came to the rescue. In 1889, Jane Addams and her partner, Ellen Starr Gates, launched Hull House. Addams was the daughter of a prosperous family whose American roots went back to the War of Independence. She was undoubtedly part of the wealthy elite. But from her early life, she was inspired to help the poor.

At first, she aspired to become a doctor. But after visiting a settlement house in England, she had the idea to create a institution like it in Chicago.

Hull House became a place where wealthy, philanthropic women lived in the city's poorest neighborhoods as residents, not as "friendly visitors." They spent time with people in poverty, both teaching and learning from them. People from different classes worked together on art and theater projects.

Even more daringly, Addams launched a research agenda to reproduce what she was doing in Chicago all over the world – in a scientific fashion. Most of the institutions addressing the poor then were places of charity, not science. There had been some important breakthroughs at hospitals and sanitariums, but the poor were never actively involved in the work. Addams engaged the very people Hull House served in co-designing new institutions to serve their own communities.

Out of this behavior — highly deviant for its time — emerged a whole class of institutions and practices that benefited the poor in ways that did not alienate or demean them. Combined with Addams's tireless advocacy, the insights generated at Hull House led to housing laws, labor laws, sanitation laws, public health reforms, playgrounds, kindergartens, juvenile courts, literacy campaigns, activism against sex trafficking, and more. Recipient of the Nobel Peace Prize in 1931, Addams is today revered as one of the mothers of the social work profession.

Jane Addams didn't eradicate every norm that led to the suffering of the poor in America's cities. Some of the norms that led to poverty at the turn of the century are still around a century later — and a few have gotten worse. But her work undoubtedly altered ideas about who ought to be included in American life and how.

Social norms like "it is okay for poor children to work in factories rather than play outside" and "women in poverty do not deserve to have children" are now almost universally condemned. And many of our other institutions, though imperfect, function in ways that are far more inclusive and just than they did a century ago.

Hull House wasn't just a program — it was the launch of a revolution in social norms.

Jane Addams set an extraordinarily high bar, but now it's time to try it yourself.

Think of a tough problem you want to solve – any problem that involves people and human behavior. This can be something you're already working on or something you think might be interesting to tackle.

Actors

▸ What people or groups are directly involved in your problem?

▸ Who influences the people or groups directly involved in your problem?

▸ Who plays an important role by not being around?

▸ What are the motivations or interests of people directly involved in your problem?

History

▸ How do people say your problem started?

▸ How do people explain why your problem is still around?

▸ What would people say are the most important events in your problem's story?

▸ What falsehoods do people spread about your problem?

Limits

▸ What are some of the rules and laws that influence how people behave around your problem?

▸ Which rules related to your problem do people usually follow and which ones do they usually ignore?

▸ How do people respond to limits of time and money related to your problem?

▸ What laws of nature are specifically related to your problem?

Future

▸ What is the most common belief about the future of your problem?

▸ What do people believe is possible, but unlikely to happen with your problem?

▸ What single event might people say would change the future of your problem?

▸ What do people believe could never, ever happen in the future of your problem?

Configuration

▸ What official labels or categories do people use when talking about your problem?

▸ What informal labels or categories do people use when talking about your problem?

▸ What labels or categories might you use when describing your problem to an outsider?

Parthood

▸ What problems are obviously related to your problem?

▸ What other problems would outsiders be surprised are related to your problem?

▸ What other problems do actors in your problem worry about?

▸ What other problems would disappear is your problem were resolved?

Norms

Now take the clues you found by answering questions on the previous six pages and piece them together to find some previously invisible social norms.

▸ What are the social situations you most associate with your problem?

▸ What do actors do in relation to your problem that can't be explained by laws or formal, explicit rules?

▸ Somebody keeps actors related to your problem in line. Who is it?

Now that you understand the whole process, here's a bonus question:

▸ Which of the norms you unearthed is problematic and keeping your problem unsolved?

Deviance

Finally, think about a behavior so powerful that it could subvert the problematic, unhealthy norm you identified.

▸ Is there an existing behavior out there that could ultimately change the norms related to your problem?

▸ Can you imagine a new behavior that could ultimately change the norms related to your problem?

We know that designing the way to solve a tough problem is not the same as solving the tough problem.

The actual solving involves lots of hard work that we don't address here at all.

But we also know that lots of hard work is wasted – and has been wasted on lots of tough problems for years or even generations – when it's in support of lousy designs and shaky strategies. Get the design right and you stand a real chance of solving the tough problem for good.

We're pulling for you.

Let us know how it goes.

You can reach Andrew at andrew@albnelson.com
and Jeff at jeff@jeffleitner.com.

About the Authors

Andrew Benedict-Nelson and Jeff Leitner have worked together regularly since 2005 on social impact projects in the United States, Europe, and Africa.

From 2010-2014, they led Insight Labs, through which they enlisted more than 600 scientists, artists, academics, and executives to rethink strategy for 45 governments, institutions and NGOs – including the U.S. Department of State, Walter Reed National Military Medical Hospital, National Endowment for the Arts, Harvard Medical School, Alfred P. Sloan Foundation, TED Conferences, Ashoka, NASA, United States National Holocaust Memorial Museum, and Community of Democracies. They also co-founded and facilitated Law 2023, a partnership with executives in the U.S. legal industry to analyze trends in technology, economics, and demographics and their future impact on the business of law.

From 2014-2018, they served together as the inaugural Innovators in Residence at the University of Southern California, in the Suzanne Dworak-Peck School of Social Work. There, they designed and helped develop the nation's first advanced practice doctorate in social innovation and the first graduate nursing program grounded in the social determinants of health. They also collaborated to develop the first systematic approach and curriculum for social innovation, which is now being taught in graduate and executive education programs.

Andrew is an adjunct professor at USC who also teaches classes and workshops in social change with partners all over the world. He studied the history of science and medicine at Northwestern University and The Johns Hopkins University. He has published book reviews and essays on these and other topics in venues such as the *Los Angeles Review of Books* and the *Times Literary Supplement*. He lives in Kansas with his wife and two dogs and a cat.

Jeff is a Bretton Woods II Fellow at New America, where he partnered with the OECD to develop the first-ever sequence for achieving the United Nations Sustainable Development Goals. He is co-founder of UX for Good, the first effort to leverage experience design to solve social problems. Jeff holds degrees from the University of Texas and The Ohio State University, and lives in Chicago with his wife and daughter.

About the Book

The authors originally developed the ideas in this book as Innovation Dynamics. The ideas themselves are grounded in millennia of others' philosophical and sociological thought – including 80-plus years of research and writings on social norms – and in the authors' own empirical observations doing social change work. This version of the text was developed in 2018 for graduate courses in social innovation at the University of Southern California.

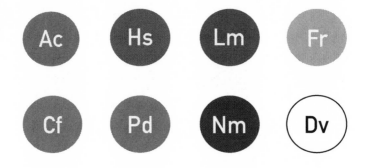

DESIGN & ICONOGRAPHY BY FOOSSA